Make Money with Membership Sites

"A guide for budding entrepreneurs who want to break into the global market through Online Marketing."

Unleashing the new way of generating Riches and passive income through Expert Membership sites!
Earn Lucrative Income from the Same Customers – Over and Over Again!"

By: **Dr. Davies M. Mulenga**

Table of Contents

1.0 An Overview on Membership Sites   **5**

    1.1 Why Start a Membership Site?   6

    1.2 Membership Sites Today   6

    1.3 Who Should Start This Membership Business?   7

    1.4 The Different Types of Membership Sites   8

2.0 Starting Your Membership Site   **10**

    2.1 Choosing Your Theme   11

    2.2 Membership Software and Scripts   11

    2.3 Using Auto Responders   12

    2.4 Deciding on Your Membership Model   13

    2.5 Deciding what Content to Use   14

    2.6 Choosing Your Publishing Schedule   15

    2.7 Suggested Membership Site Themes   16

3.0 The Free Membership Model   **17**

    3.1 Free Memberships in a Nutshell   18

    3.2 The Pros   18

    3.3 The Cons   19

    3.4 Setting up Your Free Membership – Step by Step   20

    3.5 How to Make Money   21

    3.6 Examples of Free Membership Models   22

4.0 The Paid Membership Model   **24**

    4.1 Paid Memberships in a Nutshell   25

    4.2 The Pros   25

    4.4 The Cons   26

    4.4 Setting up Your Paid Membership – Step by Step   27

    4.5 How to Make Money   28

    4.6 Examples of Paid Membership Models   29

5.0 Content For Your Membership Site   **31**

    5.1 Using Your Own Written Content   32

    5.2 Leveraging on Resell Rights   32

    5.3 Engaging Ghostwriters to Write Your Content   33

    5.4 Installing Web-Based Software   34

    5.5 Throwing in Audio and Video Products   35

6.0 Getting Members with Affiliate Programs   **37**

    6.1 The Importance of an Affiliate Program to Membership Sites   38

    6.2 How Much & How to Pay Your Affiliates?   38

    6.3 Age-Old Question: Is MLM a Viable Membership Model?   39

    6.4 Preparing Your Affiliate Marketing Materials   40

    6.5 Affiliate Hazard: Beware of Affiliate Spamming!   41

7.0 Other Marketing Methods   **43**

    7.1 Viral Marketing with E-Books   44

    7.2 Joint Ventures   45

    7.3 PPC & Search Engine Optimization   45

    7.4 Other Notable Marketing Methods   46

8.0 Managing Your Growing Membership Site   **48**

    8.1 The Importance of Offering Regular Publishing Schedules   49

    8.2 Suggestion to Improve Your Membership Site   49

    8.3 The Main Focus of Your Membership Site   50

    8.4 Being Professional with Help Desk Systems and Forums   51

    8.5 How to Manage Your Growing Members   52

9.0 In Closing   **54**

    9.1 Top Examples of Membership Sites   55

    9.2 Is Starting a Membership Site for You?   58

    9.3 Last Words and in Conclusion   58

    9.4 Recommended Resources   60

Bibliografische Information der Deutschen Nationalbibliothek:
Die Deutschen Nationalbibliothek verzeichnet diese Publikation in der Deutschen Nationalbibliografie; detaillierte Bibliografische Daten sind im Internet über http://dnb.dnb.de abrufbar.

©2019 Dr. Davies Mulenga
Herstellung und Verlag:
BoD – Books on Demand, Norderstedt

ISBN: 9783749499410

CHAPTER 1:
AN OVERVIEW ON MEMBERSHIP SITES

1.1 Why Start a Membership Site?

People are willing to pay for online content. In fact, the "Online Publishers Association" said that pay-for content is emerging as a hot revenue model. Business content, personals/match making, and entertainment are the hottest niches. But even smaller niches, like DVD authoring, sports coaching, marketing services, and dieting are producing profits.

You can sell subscriptions for online content with your own membership site? Selling online content by way of a password protected website has become big business. Not only is it fast to set up, but the start-up and running costs are minimal. Work from home entrepreneurs and big businesses alike are tapping into this newfound revenue source.

Less than nine percent of online users currently pay for online content. This means the market is wide open for the savvy entrepreneur. Paying for content in 2004 was more than 5 times what it was in 2005. That's a whopping **500%** growth! Those who capture the market first in their niche will have the obvious advantage and it's an international market, so anyone can play.

One of the great things about starting a membership site is you can take your hobby, specialized knowledge or profession and turn it into a profitable business. Your challenge will be finding exclusive content. You can start it part time but it will likely develop into a full time business.

Planning for and setting your site up for auto-responders, automated sign-ups, credit card processing, automated cancellations, etc is all part of a successful membership website. Starting and running a membership site can be a lot of fun and very exciting, however you need to know what's involved in setting one up, and then managing it effectively.

This whole process can seem a bit daunting. However, as complex as this seems, many companies offer a low cost, easy-to-use software solution. This makes it possible for almost anyone to start and market a membership site at a very low cost.

1.2 Membership Sites Today

The topics for successful member only websites are as varied today as...short people, tall people, buying websites, unusual business ideas, selling stocks, paint ball, 2nd wives clubs, financial, dating, fitness, marketing and countless mentoring and coaching sites on almost every topic imaginable and probably a few you can't imagine or wouldn't want to imagine.

It takes some work and certainly the right tools to set up a members-only website but the rewards (monetary as well as personal satisfaction) can be huge. Whatever you are passionately interested in or very adept at can be the topic of a members-only website today.

One of the first types of membership sties on the Internet was the online dating site. In the beginning, they were mostly populated with nerds, weirdoes and perverts but as the Internet matured the sites became popular among people from all walks of life. They have even progressed so far as to offer pre-screening of members. Most porn sites are membership only sites.

There are membership sites today that cover just about every area of human interests. Some offer informational or teaching material that can only be accessed by site members. Some membership can be viewed by non members but non-members are not allowed to participate in the activities or post to the message boards on the site. Sites that provide information to find work-at-home jobs, for example, can see the listing of jobs but cannot apply for the jobs unless they are members of the membership site.

There are membership sites that provide instruction is such things as how to play a guitar. The lessons are accessible only to members of the site, although those who are not members can view what subjects are being taught in the lessons.

Membership sites usually accept payment for membership fees by credit card or by personal check.

1.3 Who Should Start This Membership Business?

Anybody can start a membership business on the Internet. All that is needed is a subject, a website and the tools to build the site. The subject of the site is the real make or break issue.

A website can be obtained for as little as twelve dollars a year and the tools to build the website can be found for as little as twenty-five dollars a month. If you are going to have your website built for you, the cost will be a lot higher. However, with the tools available on the Internet, even those with limited computer skills can successfully build a website. You don't need HTML knowledge or any special skills to set up a website that can include templates, color schemes, discussion forums, blogs, a shopping cart and an auto responder.

As for the matter of choosing the topic of your membership website business, the thing to remember is that you must provide specialized information, coaching, teaching or data service that is hard to find anywhere else, or would be time consuming to find on your own. The information must be kept updated and it must be relevant to your subject. Choose a topic that you are passionate about yourself. Others will be just as passionate as you are and they are your paying membership base. The only thing left to do is to advertise your site.

After you get your website built finding or writing content is the time consuming part of a membership website that supplies information. Answering posted question on a membership website that provides instruction or teaching is a time consuming part of that type of membership website. There is no type of membership website that will not require some amount of time from you each and everyday.

1.4 The Different Types of Membership Sites

There are basically two types of membership sites. There are free sites and there are paid for sites. The two types of membership sites have one thing is common. Their memberships are made up of people who share a common interest or have a common need.

You can, of course, buy a domain, set up a website and not charge for memberships but choose who to admit and who not to admit. This is done when the profit is intended to come from sales to members after they join the site. There are free network sites that might be used for your purposes. Two examples of free membership sites are Group sites on MSN and groups on Yahoo. It costs nothing to set these sites up and there is no charge at all for a person to join. There are no paid administrators or moderators.

Each site sets its own rules for how to join and the code of conduct for the site. The site topics are many and varied. There are many "support" sites for those with health problems or concerns and for those who have suffered the loss of loved ones. There are sites for those who are passionate about crafts like quilting or woodworking. There are sites for those who love to travel. There are sites for different age groups from teens to seniors. The sites include chat software and a limited amount of space for posting pictures, documents and links per member. The free sites do not have such things as access to specialized data or lists. They don't give access to such things as music lessons.

Paid for membership sites are set up by businesses or individuals with the objective of making money by supplying hard to find information, access to specialized data or lists, or instruction in various fields. Membership sites are owned and operated by people who either own the sites or who are hired by the site owners to monitor and administer them. The topics for paid for membership sites are even more varied than the free sites and certainly more specialized.

CHAPTER 2:
STARTING YOUR MEMBERSHIP SITE

2.1 Choosing Your Theme

Choosing the theme or subject for your members-only website is a matter of personal choice and preference. Some member only sites provide mentoring or coaching, some contain useful articles or information in a particular field or product, some publish the results of tests and studies, some provide access to libraries and other reference information, some contain reviews, some provide specialized service, and some act as a meeting place for people with a common interest. The theme of your membership website needs to be something that you are passionate about or something that you have a great depth of knowledge about in order for people to be willing to pay for access to your site.

When the dot-com bubble burst, it didn't take long for the big companies to realize that there were huge amounts of money to be made by charging people for access. Such businesses as Consumer Reports and The Wall Street Journal are making millions with subscriptions to their websites. There are thousands of little guys making big bucks off membership sites as well. You won't believe some of the themes of these paid for membership websites. There are such topics as "short people, music lessons, paintball, dating services, financial, fitness, marketing, and work-at-home directories. There really isn't any subject that somewhere in the world there aren't people who would be eager to join a site to learn more about. The key to getting people to pay for access to a website, is to provide specialized information, coaching, teaching, instruction, data, or a service that is hard to find anywhere else, or would be time consuming for them to find on their own.

The bottom line is that you should choose a theme or subject for your paid-for membership website that is something you are proficient at or that you are passionate about.

2.2 Membership Software and Scripts

When you set out to create a paid for membership site, the first thing you will need to do is to buy a domain name and get a website. This is easily done and there are several places on the Internet that sell, register and host domains. One such site is GoDaddy another is CityMax. Once you have done this, the next thing you need to do is find membership software and scripts needed to build your website.

The things you need to look for when you are shopping for the software and scripts to build your website are automated signups and expirations, automated account expiration handling, an auto responder, and any other features that your website would require. You may not even be aware of all the tasks that can be automated with the right software. Tasks that take a lot of time to do by hand can b e handled automatically with software and that will free up a lot of your time to do the creative things that make your website profitable. One very good place on the Internet to get the software and script that you need is aMember Pro. The software and scripts are designed specifically for membership websites. The cost is very reasonable.

Another place on the Internet to get the software and script that you need to set up your members-only website is JVManager. This software is designed especially for Organizing Your Business, enrolling affiliates, contacting JV partners and safeguarding your products. JVManager software and script packages are about five hundred dollars per year with several payment options.

You will need specific software and specific scripts for the type of membership website you are setting up. Be certain that you enroll in the one that will provide the services that you most need to make your membership website successful.

2.3 Using Auto Responders

Be sure when you get the auto responder for your membership website that it includes a membership system. All auto responders do not have this feature and it is the one that is most important to you. Remember that there are auto responders and then there are membership based auto responders. You want the later.

All auto responders will automatically respond to email with your preset messages. All auto responders will allow you to send out preset newsletters and sales letters. However, all auto responders do not have membership systems that allow your guests to create an account and contact support about some issues and allow you to verify their email address. All auto responders are not set up to allow subscribers to join any lists from a members sign up box and, also, allow them to unsubscribe from mailings at any time. You certainly need an auto responder that will allow you to:

- Edit your profile
- Ban/or allow members
- Add members
- Edit members
- Email members
- Change the site's configuration file
- Change the site's header file
- Change the site's footer file
- Change the plan features
- View the FAQ information
- Add a global message to all members accounts

Membership sites need to be able to use their auto responders to update their member lists or their email promotions. An auto responder that has these features is what a membership site requires. An auto responder that doesn't have these features is of little use to a membership site.

In order to comply with today's anti-spam laws you need an auto responder that allow you to update your member lists and your email promotions. It also needs to have a feature that makes it easy for a member to elect to be unsubscribed and when a member does that to automatically remove them from the mailing list.

2.4 Deciding on Your Membership Model

The model you decide upon for your membership site is of the utmost importance and the one you choose depends upon your objectives. There are basically two types of membership sites. There are free sites and there are paid for sites. The two types of membership sites have one thing is common. Their memberships are made up of people who share a common need or have a common interest.

You can, of course, buy a domain, set up a website and not charge for memberships but choose who to admit and who not to admit. Or you can just set up a site on an already established network. Two examples of free membership sites are Group sites on MSN and groups on Yahoo. It costs nothing to set these sites up and there is no charge at all for a person to join.

There are no paid administrators or moderators. Each site sets its own rules for how to join and the code of conduct for the site. The site topics are many and varied. There are many "support" sites for those with health problems or concerns and for those who have suffered the loss of loved ones. There are sites for those who are passionate about crafts like quilting or wood working. There are sites for those who love to travel. There are sites for different age groups from teens to seniors. The sites include chat software and a limited amount of space for posting pictures, documents and links per member. The free sites do not have such things as access to specialized data or lists. They don't give access to such things as music lessons.

Paid for membership sites are set up by businesses or individuals with the objective of making money by supplying hard to find information, access to specialized data or lists, or instruction in various fields. Membership sites are owned and operated by people who either own the sites or who are hired by the site owners to monitor and administer them. The topics for paid for membership sites are even more varied than the free sites and certainly more specialized.

2.5 Deciding what Content to Use

The decision of what content to use on your membership site should be based on your site's theme or main topic and all content should be relevant to it. There are four different kinds of content that you can use. Each has its advantages and disadvantages. The four types of content are: written, video, audio, and web-based software solutions.

The one type of content that all websites use to some degree is written content. The written word is still the primary way of transmitting information on the Internet. What kind of written content you use is, of course, dependent upon the theme of your website. Articles, e-zines, reports, graphs, charts, etc. can all be valuable and relevant content. If you can write your own written content, it will be much better for you. If you can't, there are many places on the Internet that can supply articles, e-zines, graphs, charts, and reports for you.

Audio content is a real attention getter. Adding music...a catchy jingle or a relevant song to your website is a great content addition. It isn't really hard to do and, if you can find relevant audio, it is a good idea. Audio that provides relevant and timely information should be your main objective.

Adding video content will help you provide information to your members. Every website provides some kind of information. The object is to make the information your website provides to your membership more valuable than what other like websites are providing. Remember, though to never use technology only for the sake of technology. It needs to be a valuable addition and fit your needs.

Some membership websites can benefit from web-based software being used on their sites. Integrated content management systems (I-CMS) assist in managing enterprise documents and content. This software is particularly useful to sites that need constant updating of information.

2.6 Choosing Your Publishing Schedule

You have a membership site and people who have paid to join your site depend on you to provide relevant and timely information. They have a right to expect that information to be updated on a regular basis because they may be depending upon it to make decisions. You should state upfront what your publishing schedule will be so that members know when they can expect to get fresh information.

When you are deciding what your publishing schedule will be for your website, keep in mind the kind of information you will be supplying to your membership. If it is information that changes hourly, then you are going to need a RSS feed. Information that needs to be updated on a daily basis will most likely require a content management system. For weekly publishing of content, you can do that yourself but a content management system can make it a lot easier.

When planning your newsletter, you need to decide how often your e-zine will be sent out to your subscribers. Essentially, you need to create a schedule and stick with it. But how often should you publish? How much is too much and how often is not enough? When it comes to frequency, the usual choices are daily, weekly, bi-weekly, or monthly.

- Daily - that means 365 newsletters a year. You could wear out your welcome even with your most devoted members.

- Weekly - that is still a lot of work...52 letters a year... a little over 4 a month. Would your members appreciate that much mail from you?

- Bi-weekly - Publishing an e-zine twice a month is just often enough to keep you fresh in your subscribers' minds but not so often that they become annoyed with you.

- Monthly - doesn't seem often enough. Your members may forget about you and where your website lives on the Internet.

2.7 Suggested Membership Site Themes

When you are deciding on the theme for your membership site, it is best if you can choose a theme that concerns something you are really interested in...even passionate about. Remember that you will be spending a lot of time keeping your membership informed, keeping your website interesting and keeping relevant and timely content on your website and in your e-zine that you send out regularly.

If you choose to start a membership site about...say... dogs. Just **dogs** in general won't attract many members. You will need to choose a specific breed... and possibly even narrow it down further. Instead of Poodles, your theme should be; Tiny Toy Poodles, Miniature Poodles, or Standard Poodles, for example. Millions of people are dog lovers and the theme of a specific breed of dog should do well.

If you are really into video or computer **games**, start a membership site devoted to one specific game... not just video games or computer games in general. People all over the world and from every walk of life get really involved with a specific video or computer game and love to talk to others about the game and give each other hints.

There are thousands...maybe millions...of people who love **certain crafts and hobbies.** However, those who love to quilt aren't interested in wood working so your membership site should be about a specific craft or hobby.

Professionals like to talk to other professionals in the same field. Each professional field speaks their own language and find the same things to be interesting, informative or funny. So if you start a membership site for professionals, you should get a good response.

A membership website with the theme, '**Resell Rights**', should do well, also. This kind of site will need to be kept updated on a regular basis.

CHAPTER 3:
THE FREE MEMBERSHIP MODEL

3.1 Free Memberships in a Nutshell

Basically, a free membership site is a site where the user is not charged a membership fee to use the site but is required to supply their e-mail address, choose a user name and password to enter the site, participate in the discussions and activities. Sometimes free memberships are limited to less useful information or access while paid memberships have full access.

A large entity like MSN, for example, allows members to access most things on their sites without the need for any sign in procedure at all but, in order to join a group, you must supply your email address, choose a user name and a password. The use of the site is still free. However, to use MSN as your ISP or to gain enhanced email resources you will be required to pay for it.

In the same way, an individual might start a free membership website. There would be no charge at all to access the site. To gain access to limited information would require supplying an email address, choosing a user name and a password. To gain full access to the site would most likely require payment if the information they are providing merits a fee. Some sites never charge a membership fee and rely solely on selling their own product or promoting products produced by others as a source of income.

Free membership sites very rarely, if ever, supply information that you couldn't easily acquire on the Internet yourself. An individual who sets up a free membership site doesn't do it for free so they will be planning to make an income in some way. Usually free membership sites are for the purpose of selling a product or service. Some information will be provided but supplying information is not the main objective.

3.2 The Pros

Free membership sites do have their advantages. When you start setting up your membership website, ask yourself what your main objective is. If your main objective is supplying information that is not readily available or easily found anywhere, then your site should not be a free site. If, on the other hand, the main objective of your website is to sell your own product or products that others have produced, then a free website might be exactly what you are looking for.

Free online membership products and services are very popular. In fact the most recent estimates from June 2005 indicate that nearly 45,000 membership products or services are being marketed online, and there are more than 120 million subscribers to online products and services in the United States alone.

If the theme of your website is, say, Toy Poodles, you might have a message board, blog, or forum where people who have and love Toy Poodles could meet and discuss them, as well as, articles and information about Toy Poodles for all members to view. However, your objective would be to sell products you advertise that relate to Toy Poodles. Your income would be derived from the sale of the products and not from fees charged for memberships.

Free membership websites require much less time to administer than do paid membership sites. The content is generally much easier to find and to write. The members themselves supply a lot of content just with their posts. It's easy to hold interest by running picture contests or doing online quizzes that are easy and quick to get up and running.

When you sell products rather than memberships, there is no need for a customer support system. This alone eliminates a lot of the time, work and aggravation of managing a website.

3.3 The Cons

If there is an upside, there is always a downside to everything including free membership websites. Your free membership website that you have set up is supposed to practically run itself. It isn't supposed to eat up large chunks of your time, is it?

You have to monitor the blogs, forums and message boards constantly to keep material off that is offensive to most of your members...even if they don't pay you a dime to do it. Even though you aren't making anything from people being able to post on your website, state their thoughts and even vent, you are still responsible for what is posted. Unless you are running an adult content website where anything and everything goes, you have to spend a lot of time just monitoring the website.

In order to maintain enough interest and keep enough traffic flowing through your website you have to keep relevant, timely and interesting content on your site even if your main objective is to see products and not entertain or inform the public.

You must publish an e-zine at least bi-weekly in order to keep your members informed and interested. Writing content for your newsletter is a time consuming task and pays nothing up front.

You must guard against spamming your members. Complying with anti-spam legislation is important. No matter how sure you are of the worth of the products you are selling, you still aren't allowed to spam your members. You will find them opting out of your site in droves if your over-do your advertising.

Another not-so-good-thing that happens to a free membership site owner is that a product that you are advertising turns out to be a dud. Now you have an irate member who will tell others on the site about the product that failed to live up to what was promised. You must constantly be on the look out for these kinds of posts to your forums or blogs and take immediate steps to set things right.

3.4 Setting up Your Free Membership – Step by Step

You have decided to set up a free membership website. Good for you. Now you need to take these steps in order to accomplish the task of getting your website up and running.

Step #1: Decide on the theme of your site.

What will be the main subject that will be discussed or the main item that will be sold on your website? This is the first decision that needs to be made because almost everything else will depend on this decision.

Step #2: Choose a name for your website.

Here you need to make a list of several different names that would describe what the main objective of your website and its theme is. Put the ones that have fewer than 20 letters in them at the top of your list.

Step#3: Find out what names are available.

Go to GoDaddy or find and do a search beginning with the names you have chosen that have the fewest number of letters in them. Search until you find a suitable domain name.

Step #4: Register the domain name.

Step #5: Get a webhost.

There are many good ones. Do a Google search to find one that will meet your needs.

Step #6: Install membership management software on the web server.

You can find great membership management software. Again...do a Google search to find it.

Step #7: Install a CMS on the server to manage content.

Another Google search is in order. You need relevant and timely content.

Step #8: Add content.

Remember, all content, whether it is written, audio or video content, needs to be relevant to the theme of your website.

Step #9: Set up payment processing.

This is done on sites like Paypal or ClickBank. You need this whether you are selling memberships or merchandize.

Step #10 Launch the site.

That is, start running advertisements to attract members.

3.5 How to Make Money

Even though you don't charge for memberships to your website, there are still many ways to make a profit from it. You must first, however, attract members by having a theme and promoting your site and then providing good, relevant and timely information, and having a blog and/or a message board or a forum. And you must harvest email addresses as members sign up. Then here are a few ideas of how to make some money:

Idea #1: Sell your own product.

This can be a physical product or an e-book, report, how-to instructions or e-zines that your members would be interested in.
If you build bird houses, for example, you can sell them on your free membership site with a theme of 'birds'. If you can give guitar lessons, you sell the lessons on your site with a theme of 'guitars'.

Idea #2: Sell products that others produce.

These can be 'real' world products or e-books, reports, how-to instructions or e-zines. The advertisements for these products are on your website and when members click on the ads, you are paid for a lead or a percentage of the sale of the item. An example of this would be if you have a free membership site with a theme of 'birds' you could have advertisements of birdhouses built by others or bird feeders built by others. When your members click on the ads and purchase the products you make money.

Idea #3: You can sell advertising space on your website for products related to your theme.

You won't make a profit off the sale but you will get paid for advertising the product.

Idea #4: Some companies will pay you to endorse their products in your e-zine.

This is not just an advertisement. It is a personal endorsement by you that recommends the product.

3.6 Examples of Free Membership Models

There are thousands of free membership sites on the Internet. So, just what exactly do these free membership websites do to earn money? Well, you see, the Internet has totally revolutionized our world. Today, one person armed with a computer, an idea and a few dollars can create an online presence that rivals those of multi-million dollar companies.

You've got one man (or woman) on a computer selling a top-quality product to visitors - throughout the world - who are quick to assume the company has an office building and multiple employees. But in reality, it's one person, working from home, generating enormous profits. Truly, the Internet represents a level playing field for the sole-proprietor looking to start a subscription website. It is really amazing that one lone individual with an idea and a few dollars can compete with huge corporations that have a zillion dollars to spend on advertising alone... but, even though it sounds too good to be true, it is true.

The old way of making money from free membership sites was to harvest email addresses and sell them to the highest bidder. That old method has pretty much gone the way of the horse and buggy. Today's computer users are way too savvy to just give up their email addresses without a guarantee that they won't be sold or rented. The new anti-spam laws were the final nails in the coffin of harvesting email addresses to sell.

Two examples of successful free membership web businesses are:

The Viral Marketing Vault - This is a free membership site, owned by David Thompson, which promises not to sell your email address and provides valuable marketing information to its members.

Outsource Secrets - the secrets of outsourcing effectively on the free membership site.

CHAPTER 4:
THE PAID MEMBERSHIP MODEL

4.1 Paid Memberships in a Nutshell

Whatever you call them - member only, membership, subscription, or mentor websites, they all have one thing in common. They are bringing in steady and constant cash flow for their owners, month after month, from a few hundred dollars to tens of thousands of dollars. The array of the topics of these websites is endless.

Some of these paid membership sites provide mentoring or coaching, others publish useful articles or information in a particular field or product. Still others publish the results of tests and studies or product reviews. Some membership sites provide specialized service or act as a meeting place for people with a common interest and then there are those that provide step-by-step instructions for such things as painting or music.

All these sites have one thing in common: to access the website (or the best information on the site) you have to pay for it! Which begs the question...why would anybody pay for information on the Internet?

The answer is simple. People buy information that they could probably find for themselves if they looked long enough and hard enough, because they want to save time or because they think the information will be better or more specialized or because the information just isn't available to them unless they pay for it.

Just a few short years ago it was almost unheard of to charge for access to a website and almost no one was doing it. Today, however, it is the norm and not the exception. Actually we have Internet dating sites to thank for this huge money making opportunity.

The Internet dating industry began with free membership sites that were mostly populated by nerds, weirdoes and perverts. It was quickly discovered that ordinary people would gladly pay to have access to lists where the posters had been screened even just a little. Now people actually expect to pay for access to valuable information.

4.2 The Pros

A successful member only, paid membership site is one of the best ways to make money online. A successful membership site can produce a steady income comparable to that of a successful corporate executive but without the job. This is the biggest advantage to a paid membership website owner. It provides a recurring stream of income, and a steady, reliable source of money month after month. The steady stream of income provided by such a concept has led many people to abandon the old one time sale model in favor of this more dynamic approach.

Let's say if you had just 200 people paying you just $20.00 a month, you would have a steady cash flow of $4000.00/month, month after month, rain or shine. Many people accomplish this the first month or two their site is up. But that's just the beginning. Some individuals have member only websites that generate many times that amount of money. People are eagerly seeking information, and they will gladly pay for what they perceive as more valuable, reliable content-because they paid for it!

One huge advantage a paid membership site has over a free membership site is that the money is paid to the owner up-front and doesn't depend on sales or advertising income after a person joins the site.

Paid membership sites that sell memberships to access information based products have a huge advantage over those that promote physical goods. Unlike hard goods, information based products require no storage, no warehousing and no handling. There are no shipping charges to worry about, and it costs nothing to store such products.

In addition, once those products have been created, they can be sold over and over again and sold to many different members. All that the Internet entrepreneur needs to do is market those products effectively.

4.3 The Cons

Unfortunately, every human endeavor that has an upside always has a downside. That is just one of the hard cold facts of life and paid membership sites are no exception to the rule. There are some disadvantages of having a paid membership website...not many...but there are some disadvantages.

The biggest disadvantage of a paid membership site is the continuing problem of content for the website. When members subscribe to a website and pay money to access information, they expect that information to be very valuable and even exclusive. It can't be information they could get by simply typing in a few words to their favorite search engine and getting a zillion hits. Writing original, relevant and timely information pertaining to whatever the theme of your paid membership website is can require a massive amount of time. Audio or audio/video content can require even more time... not to mention expense.

But content is the key to membership renewals. If you don't invest the time required to keep your content up-to-date and relevant, you will not get the renewals that you need to keep getting that regular income.

Another disadvantage of a paid membership website is that the message boards, forums and blogs that are associated with a paid membership site must be monitored carefully and updated regularly.

People who pay for a membership to a website expect to get what they are paying for...actually they usually expect to get more than what they are paying for. It is imperative that the owner of a paid membership website schedule chats with experts in the field that is the theme of the website on a regular basis and that the owner of the website be available to answer questions at certain times of everyday.

The bottom line is the biggest disadvantage of a paid membership website is that the owner of such a site must be willing to invest a lot of time.

4.4 Setting up Your Paid Membership – Step by Step

So you have decided to set up a paid membership website. You are willing to invest whatever time you need to invest because you are so passionate about your subject. That's great! You already have your theme and now you need to take these steps in order to accomplish the task of getting your website up and running.

Step #1: Choose a name for your website.

Here you need to make a list of several different names that would describe what the main objective of your website and its theme is. Put the ones that have fewer than 20 letters in them at the top of your list.

Step#2: Find out what names are available.

Go to Godaddy or find and do a search beginning with the names you have chosen that have the fewest number of letters in them. Search until you find a suitable domain name.

Step #3: Register the domain name.

Step #4: Get a web hosting account.

There are many good ones. Do a Google search to find one that will meet your needs.

Step #5: Install membership management software on the web server.

You can find great membership management software. Again...do a Google search to find it.

Step #6 Add content.

Remember, all content, whether it is written, audio or video content, needs to be relevant to the theme of your website. Since you are starting a paid membership site about something you are passionate about, you should have a lot of content ready but remember that content must be kept up dated.

Step #7: Set up payment processing.

This is done on sites like Paypal or ClickBank. You need this whether you are selling memberships, merchandize or both.

Step #8 Launch the site.

That is, start running advertisements to attract members.

4.5 How to Make Money

Initial income from a paid membership site is, of course, the paid subscriptions to the site but that just isn't all the income that is available to the owner of a paid subscription site.

Renewals: Recurring income is one of the best parts of running a membership website, and something that many other types of online businesses lack. While most types of Internet businesses survive by selling a couple of products, they must rely on selling large quantities of those products month after month. The owner of a paid membership site doesn't have to worry about selling products every month but they do have to be concerned with membership renewals. While first time subscribers certainly breathe life into a membership website, renewals keep it alive, well and producing ongoing income. This is why content is so important on a paid membership site.

Selling advertising space: Owners of paid membership websites can sell advertising space on the site to companies that sell products related to the theme of the website. This is an excellent way to add income and one overlooked by many owners of membership websites. Simply contact the companies who sell products related to the site and offer to sell advertising space that will be seen by people who will be most interested in the products they are selling.

Sending endorsement emails: Offers to companies that sell products that are related to the theme of a website can be made for endorsements of their products in the email, e-zine, or newsletters that are sent to the membership list. If the owner of the membership site has established himself as an expert in the field, companies are willing to pay for personal endorsements of related products because members will have faith in the website owner's knowledge and expertise.

4.6 Examples of Paid Membership Models

In today's global market place the door stands wide open for those who are willing to walk through it. Less than nine percent of online users currently pay for online content. This means the market is wide open for the savvy entrepreneur. Paying for content in 2005 was more than 5 times what it was in 2004. That's a whopping 500% growth! Those who capture the market first in their niche obviously have an advantage but it's an international market, so anyone can play.

There are paid membership sites today that cover just about every area of human interests. Some offer informational or teaching material that can only be accessed by site members. Some membership sites can be viewed by non members but non-members are not allowed to participate in the activities or post to the message boards on the site. Sites that provide information to find work-at-home jobs, for example, can see the listing of jobs but cannot apply for the jobs unless they are members of the membership site.

Three examples of very successful paid membership websites that are alive, well and making money on the Internet this very minute are:

Marketing Main Event: This is a fine example of paid membership website marketing at its best and with a twist. In the beginning memberships were limited to the first 1000 paid memberships...at the moment down to 350 and memberships allow access to very specific information.

Resell Rights Mastery: This is another excellent example of a paid membership website that is marketing with a twist. This twist is that the memberships are available only by invitation.

Another example of a profitable paid membership site that is not business related is:

[Guitar Lessons with Video](): This website offers a free download that includes three open chords plus some seventh and minor chords. The full beginner course and access to a forum and blog must be bought.

CHAPTER 5:
CONTENT FOR YOUR MEMBERSHIP SITE

5.1 Using Your Own Written Content

Using your own written content for your members-only website is by far the best thing that you can do. Not only will you have great content for your own website but you can use original articles and e-books to advertise your site as well.

If you have a talent for writing, then, by all means, always write your own content for your website. You can choose all of the subject matter yourself and write it in a way that will be the best way to present the material to your subscribers. Nobody knows better than you what your member want to know and how they would most want to see the material presented.

The advantage of writing all written content for your members-only website is that you can include the links that are most valuable to you personally....links to product sales pages, for example, that you have a monetary interest in. You also have the option of endorsing products that you get paid for endorsing which is yet another source of income.

There are a few important things that you should know about writing web content. Even if you have written copy for years, writing web copy is a bit different. People who read information presented on the Internet do not read word by word. They scan an article. Therefore, it is of the utmost importance that your headline is an attention grabber or they won't read the information at all. Since people who read information on the Internet scan the other important things to remember when writing your own content are:

- Important words and phrases need to be put in bold type or highlighted.
- Highlight key words and sub-titles.
- Use only one idea per paragraph.
- Make use of bulleted lists.

5.2 Leveraging on Resell Rights

Creating a product is usually one of the first concerns of an Internet marketer. Thinking up a profitable idea and making a marketing plan to sell it is really exhausting work. Not everyone is gifted with the creativity to come up with a brand new product. That's why resell rights came into existence.

Internet marketers sell their created products for one of two reasons; either because they have squeezed them dry of all possible earning potential, or they think that they'll earn more by selling the master rights to them. This has paved the way for resale rights marketing, which is an ingenious method of making profit out of what others' have created.

Here are a few ways to leverage on resell rights:

1. Re-brand, repackage, resell: If the resale rights marketer holds the master rights to the product, he could name himself as the author, change a few things here and there, and sell the product as something new.
2. Buy and sell: The resale rights marketer can also make use of the most fundamental principle of profit: buy low, sell high.
3. Divide before distributing: An e-book can be broken down to a series of articles which can be used as auto-responders, e-zine or newsletter content, or chapters for other e-books.
4. Use it as a free gift: A way to leverage resell rights is to use it as a freebie, or package it with other e items to justify a higher price.
5. Auction it off: This would allow the reseller to earn more than what he originally paid for the e-book.

There are so many ways that a reseller can leverage profits and add website content when he buys resell rights to a well-written e-book. The ways are limited only by the reseller's imagination.

5.3 Engaging Ghostwriters to Write Your Content

First, what exactly is a ghostwriting? Ghostwriting is actually a very simple agreement where an individual or company hires a writer to create a work that will be owned outright by the buyer. The buyer is not required to give credit to the writer and is even allowed to claim authorship.

Ghostwriting is perfectly legal. Ghostwriting has been around a long time. Some of the most famous and influential leaders have used others to write their speeches or even autobiographies. Ghostwriters do not hold any copyrights to the finished work. This is also known as a 'work-for-hire' arrangement.

E-business owners find that lack of time and lack of writing ability often leads them to considering the assistance of a ghostwriter for original content on their websites. The Internet is based on written information. Special talent is needed to convey information clearly or to create readable books (or e-books) for customers or visitors to a website. By passing this job to a qualified ghostwriter an e-business owner will save time and increase profits or customer satisfaction by providing information that has been written in a professional way.

There are many sources online for finding ghostwriters. You can find them on a bidding site (like elance.com or rentacoder.com), from a personal website or from a ghostwriting service site. If you plan on using a ghostwriter on a regular basis, it might be wise to develop a relationship with a freelancer as opposed to using a ghostwriting service from a company who manages the relationship for you.

It is important to remember that when you are hiring a ghostwriter, you are hiring talent. Taking the time to find out whether a particular ghostwriter can produce work that will be valuable to you is well worth your time and effort.

5.4 Installing Web-Based Software

Installing web-based software (such as an auto responder) on your members-only site is a very simple matter, indeed. All you must do is sign up and pay for an auto responder service at one of the many sites online. There are free auto responders but they put their ads on every message that is sent out. If you are going to have members pay you for the use of the auto responder, you should get one that is paid for and not a free one.

On the other hand you might just want to make use of sites that let you use their auto responders. One such site is aWeber. There is a big concern in email marketing circles about mail deliverability, which refers to whether emails sent (broadcast) to your lists make it through. The problem is a lot of mail servers block mass emails sent out and unless the email responder service provider has pre-arranged to be white listed your mail won't get through. That's pretty detrimental to any online company. AWeber has the enviable record of the highest percentage of email deliverability.

Other software that you could install on your membership-only website are html editors or WYSIWIG editors to help your members create web pages. Depending on the site, various tools like calculators could be installed to benefit members.

Another good site to look at that can help you with installing web-based software is SOLOBIS. It's a sad fact that the setting up and marketing a successful Internet Business is beyond the reach of most people. The problems are many; from a lack of knowledge of powerful business and marketing concepts, to not knowing how to start, to not being technically proficient, to not knowing who the right people are to approach for help, and of course, the lack of money.

5.5 Throwing in Audio and Video Products

You can enhance your members-only website by adding some audio and video products that will inform or entertain your members.

With pod casting you can do your blogging and online diary entries with sound now. Think of what pod casting could mean for your website. With pod casting readers can now get to know you at a new level. Many people like to listen to sound files and would rather listen to a pod casting blog than read a long written blog.

You can do pod casting easily. Record your pod casting blog and put it on your site or use a pod casting service to host your pod casting blogs. Then your readers can listen to your pod casting blogs instead of read your written blogs.

They can also download your pod casting blogs onto their Ipod or MP3 player and listen to what you have to say while they're doing something else. If you use a pod casting hosting service they can subscribe to your pod casting blog and every time you update it they will receive a notice.

If you would like to record your own audio messages to use on your website, download Audacity (it's free).

Simply follow the directions, record what you want to say and upload it onto your site.

Video is a bit more complicated but it can be done. There are three main video file types that you will encounter on the Web: QuickTime, AVI, and MPEG. MPEG and QuickTime are most commonly found. QuickTime is the most popular.

RSS feeds to your website will supply both audio and video content. Putting RSS feed links into you web page allows headlines and summary content sourced from other blogs to display on your web pages.

When the blog content is updated, your pages are updated. This gives them characteristics that search engines find attractive.

CHAPTER 6:
GETTING MEMBERS WITH AFFILIATE PROGRAMS

6.1 The Importance of an Affiliate Program to Membership Sites

Affiliate programs are important to membership sites for a number of good reasons. An affiliate program isn't really a program. It's a business arrangement.
Affiliate programs are also known as associate programs, associates programs, referral programs and even bounty programs. Most affiliate programs are free to join. Affiliate programs are a way to earn money without producing your own product.

Affiliate programs allow a membership website to generate additional (other than the membership subscription) income by advertising products that are relevant to the site's theme. For example, let's say you own a membership website whose theme is golf. You would recommend products that you like yourself like golf books, magazines, videos and golfing gear. When you have an affiliate agreement with the merchants selling those products, they provide you with affiliate links which you paste into your site. Then when members click on those links and buy those products, you earn a commission. Affiliates programs can earn commissions in three ways: per click, per sale and per lead.

The members on a membership website are helped by the affiliate programs as well. They are given easy access to products that they would otherwise have to search the Internet to find.

On the other side of the aisle, you can let other companies post your ad on their sites and pay commissions for sales of your product or memberships. Sure, you may give away 10 percent of your profit to an affiliate; but 90 percent of something is better than 100 percent of nothing. You'll make up in sales quantity what you may lose in percentage of your own net. It's quite worthwhile in the long run.

Use your e-zine to advertise your affiliate program. Always encourage your newsletter subscribers to forward the newsletter to a friend.

6.2 How Much & How to Pay Your Affiliates

Different companies pay different percentages and amounts for leads and sales. The differences paid for a sale can range from 75% down to 1% depending on the company and the product. What you decide to pay your affiliates will depend entirely upon what you are selling and to whom you are selling it. A good idea would be to check what other companies selling a product comparable to yours is paying their affiliates. However, how much you pay your Affiliates really depends on how much your product/service costs, its profit margin, how much you're willing to give up and what action you want to take place.

Let's say that your product is priced at $100.00. Let's also assume that it cost you $10.00 to make it. This leaves you with $90.00 profit is you sell it yourself. The question is how much of this do you want to give away to the person that made this sale possible? Let's say you offer 50% to your affiliates. It still costs you $10.00 to produce the product so now you will be making $40 profit on the sale. A lot less for sure but 40 is better than the nothing you would have made without the sale.

The other problem is how to pay your affiliates. Money exchanging hands on the Internet presents a whole new set of problems, doesn't it? However, that problem has been solved for you. Paypal is set up to handle receiving, as well as, sending payments and it takes the money exchange problem out of the equation. When a Paypal account is set up, the bank account of an individual or company is verified, as well as, their credit card information. Paypal provides a quick, safe, easy and secure way to transfer monies between individuals and companies.

6.3 Age-Old Question Is MLM a Viable Membership Model?

If you think you want to get involved with MLM, do your research first. The challenge with MLM businesses is that people at the top are most often the winners. The biggest majority of people at the bottom end up spending money and time to get involved and end up losing whatever they put in. Multi-level marketing (MLM) is a marketing and distribution structure. People at the top sell to those below them, who in turn sell to those below them. The higher up you are in this structure, the more money you can make. Be sure to check with at least a few other people who've entered at your level (who you identify on your own, separate from people the MLM promoter refers you to), and see what they have to say. Find out what they have to say on how - and if it's possible - to be successful.

There are advantages to Multi-level marketing. First, the start up cost is usually very low and that is a big plus to the work-at-home mom (for example) who has limited funds to launch an online business. It is a way to get started in an online business with a very small personal investment and that is a very appealing thing for many people. Pre-packaged tools and products are provided and that saves a lot of money and relieves the need for warehousing.

Also, sales techniques are given and for the newbie to Internet marketing this is a very attractive advantage.

There are also disadvantages to Multi-level marketing. Many (if not most) people lose money in MLM activities, because they can't sell the product as effectively as they thought they could. And then there is the problem of credibility. It can become an issue, especially if you start treating friends like they're customers.

6.4 Preparing Your Affiliate Marketing Materials

There are at least forty affiliate directories providing searchable database's to help webmasters find affiliate programs suitable for their sites. Think of them as the Google of the affiliate world.

Each directory has their own submission policies but in general they will not accept adult or porn sites, or a MLM (a company that pays commissions on more than 2-tiers. Many won't accept gambling sites and most won't accept submissions from affiliates themselves, submits need to come from the program owner.

In every case a submission will be reviewed by the directories editors before it is included in the directory. Also keep in mind that they are very busy and if you have taken any shortcuts in the submission process of not abided by all submission policies the chances are your request will just be deleted from the submission list without further ado.

1. Make sure your program is ready and that everything works properly. Make sure there are no little red crosses where logos and banners should be and spell-check your pages.

2. Create your own affiliate information page and include:
   - A description of your product/service
   - Illustrate your commission and payment terms
   - Make sure the programs terms and conditions are available before joining.
   - Include a link to your home page and privacy policy

3. Look at the category choices to find the most suitable to submit your program to. Try to search as an affiliate might. Some headings can have more than one meaning.

4. Plan out the data you want to submit. If you're only given the option to provide one address, submit that of your affiliate information page. Write your program description. You will also need a list of keywords or key phrases, comma separated. Choose phrases affiliates might use to search out your product/service types or program features.

6.5 Affiliate Hazard: Beware of Affiliate Spamming!

The modern variation of the practice of paying finder's-fees for the introduction of new clients to a business is a popular method of promoting Internet businesses called affiliate marketing. An affiliate marketer is paid for every visitor, subscriber, or customer provided to an Internet business because of his efforts. The affiliate marketer earns compensation based on a certain value for each visit (Pay per click), registrant (Pay per lead), or a commission for each customer or sale (Pay per Sale), or any combination.

You can see where an affiliate marketer would be sorely tempted to send out email advertising the products he makes money on for promoting. This resulted in so much SPAM being generated that anti-spam laws were enacted.

Spammers are severely fined and the newest twist in the anti-spam laws are that the merchants whose affiliates spam are being held responsible for the spamming as well. So caution is well advised to merchants.

Merchants who are considering adding an affiliate strategy to their online sales channel should research the different technological solutions available to them. As affiliate marketing has matured many affiliate merchants have refined their terms and conditions to prohibit affiliates from spamming. Some types of affiliate management solutions include: standalone software, hosted services, shopping carts with affiliate features, and third party affiliate networks.

Spamdexing or search engine spamming is the practice of deliberately creating web pages which will be indexed by search engines in order to increase the chance of a website or page being placed close to the beginning of search engine results, or to influence the category to which the page is assigned.

Right now there is a lot of debate about the affiliate practice of Spamdexing and many affiliates have converted from sending email spam to creating large volumes of automatically generated web pages each devoted to different niche keywords as a way of search engine optimizing their sites. This is sometimes referred to as spamming the search engine results. Spam is the biggest threat to organic Search Engines whose goal is to provide quality search results for keywords or phrases entered by their users.

CHAPTER 7:
OTHER MARKETING METHODS

7.1 Viral Marketing with E-Books

Promoting your site by producing an electronic book is a great idea. This viral marketing technique is not only very clever but is very effective. You produce the book, then allow others to distribute it from their own sites and e-zines without charging them anything.

Producing an e-book is a relatively simple matter. You write and/or gather together between 10 and 20 articles. Less than 10 articles is not really enough of an e-book to attract much attention, and more than 20 makes for a large download. Remember to include enough material to make an interesting book, but not so much that those people with dial-up connections can't download it in a few minutes.

Next put together a nicely formatted e-book with a table of contents. Be sure to include hyperlinks to your web site all over - at least one per page. Also, you can include brief advertisements, links to join your newsletter and all kinds of other things.

Remember what you are doing is creating something that you want people to put up on their web sites, send to their friends and recommend to everyone. So, while you want to promote your website and your products, be sure the e-book is valuable enough that people really want it. The people you want to recommend your e-book don't want to recommend you or your products, they want to recommend the content of your e-book.

Advertise, advertise, advertise your new e-book. Post it on your web site, promote it in your e-zine and add a link to your e-mail signature. You can sell it if you want - or you can just give it away. Give everyone permission to post it, send it, copy it and sell it as much as they want. In fact, it would be a good idea to have the first page explain what you are up to. Tell people what they can do with the e-book, don't make it a secret.

Assuming you've created a great e-book, just give it some time. It takes time for a virus to spread and it will take some time for your viral e-book to spread. Just keep remembering that each and every copy will have your links, your products and your site mentioned. That can add up to a lot of traffic - for free.

7.2 Joint Ventures

Setting up joint ventures with established Internet marketers could be your key to real profits and the quickest way of making a profit on the Internet. You could, or course, set up your own affiliate program for your product or service and get up an army of sales people to work for you, but partnering up with established Internet marketers will make for faster sales. The reason is simple. It's reputation. By setting up joint ventures with established players, you will be partnering up with individuals who have developed trusting relationships with thousands of their own customers and readers.

Setting up a joint venture is a relatively easy thing to do. You simply find the individuals who have developed a strong reputation and who can reach a lot of people then ask them to endorse your product. These people could be the publishers of the e-zines you subscribe to on a regular basis or a web site that compliments your product or service. These are the people you need to help endorse your product! In exchange for endorsing your product, they get a cut of the profits... but part of something is better than all of nothing.

If you have a web site that generates a lot of traffic or an e-zine with a lot of readers, you can contact the owner of a product or service and offer to endorse it for a cut of the profits because joint ventures can also work in the other direction.
 If they already run an existing affiliate program, you can even justify a higher commission based on the number of sales you will bring him or her. Most of these businesses will not hesitate to give you a bigger commission if you can generate more sales for them.

A joint venture with other e-zine publishers is also good way to increase the circulation of your own opt-in list.

7.3 PPC & Search Engine Optimization

Placement of the advertisement for your website in search engine results is at least partially based on how many clicks are made on your ad. However, there are many things that affect the rankings of a website, hence, the coming-of-age of companies that do search engine optimization (SEO) for a fee. Professional search engine optimization services are not expensive and yet they can make a huge difference to any web site or blog, in terms of the traffic and ultimately the revenue they receive.

The most important thing that professional search engine optimization company or individual should be able to do is dramatically increase traffic by ensuring that your web site is highly visible through a prominent page ranking. A prominent page ranking will mean that your web site will score high again and again during searches which will in turn guarantee that a sizeable number of the people carrying out searches using various key words, end up visiting your web site. This can translate into tens of thousands and sometimes hundreds of thousands of visitors every month. If even a small percentage become customers then you win.

However, it takes a really professional SEO service to keep your website high in the rankings because search engines make frequent adjustments and changes to how pages are ranked. All prospective users should ask any professional SEO firm or individual for tangible evidence of their success through references. If the SEO firm or individual is any good they will be glad to provide references to you. If they don't provide references keep looking until you find a company or individual who will. Do not take the references at face value. Contact these past or current clients and ask them questions about their level of satisfaction with the SEO firm or individual you are considering.

7.4 Other Notable Marketing Methods

Effectively promoting your website is the key to a successful Internet business... no matter what that business is. There are the obvious ways like, writing a great e-book that contains links to your site and products, that you give away and joining in on joint ventures with established Internet marketers. There are other ways to promote you website, however, and here are just a few ideas that might help:

Promote Your Site in Online Forums and Blogs. The Internet offers thousands of very targeted e-mail based discussion lists, online forums, blogs, and Usenet news groups made up of people with very specialized interests. Use Google, MSN or Yahoo Groups to find appropriate sources. Don't bother with news groups consisting of pure spam. Instead, find groups where a serious dialog is taking place. Don't use aggressive marketing and overtly plug your product or service. Rather, add to the discussion in a helpful way and let the signature at the end of your e-mail message do your marketing for you. People will gradually get to know and trust you, visit your site, and do business with you.

Announce a Contest. People like getting something free. If you publicize a contest or drawing available on your site, you'll generate more traffic than normal. Make sure your sweepstakes rules are legal in all states and countries you are targeting. Prizes should be designed to attract individuals who fit a demographic profile describing your best customers.

Exchange Ads with Complementary Businesses. Banner exchange programs don't work well these days. But consider exchanging e-mail newsletter ads with complementary businesses to reach new audiences. Just be sure that your partners are careful where they get their mailing list or you could be in trouble with the CAN-SPAM Act.

Devise Viral Marketing Promotion Techniques. So-called viral marketing uses the communication networks of your site visitors or customers to spread the word about your site. Word-of-mouth, PR, creating "buzz," and network marketing are offline model.

Buy a Text Ad in an E-Mail Newsletter. Some of the best buys are small text ads in e-mail newsletters targeted at audiences likely to be interested in your products or services. Many small publishers aren't sophisticated about advertising and offer attractive rates.

CHAPTER 8:
MANAGING YOUR GROWING MEMBERSHIP SITE

8.1 The Importance of Offering Regular Publishing Schedules

The people who have paid to join your membership site depend on you to provide relevant and timely information. It is their right to expect that information to be updated on a regular basis because they may be depending upon it to make decisions. When a person joins your membership site they should be told what your publishing schedule will be so that they know when they can expect to get fresh information. Adhering to that announced schedule is vitally important.

Deciding what your publishing schedule will be for your website is important. Keep in mind the kind of information you will be supplying to your membership. Information that changes hourly will require a RSS feed. Information that needs to be updated on a daily basis will most likely require a content management system. For weekly publishing of content, you can do that yourself but a content management system can make it a lot easier.

When you are planning your newsletter, you need to decide how often your e-zine or newsletter will be sent out to your subscribers. Basically, you need to create a schedule and stick with it. But how often should you publish? How much is too much and how often is not enough? When it comes to frequency, the usual choices are daily, weekly, bi-weekly, or monthly.

- Daily...that means 365 newsletters a year. You could wear out your welcome even with your most devoted members.
- Weekly...that is still a lot of work...52 letters a year...a little over 4 a month. Would your members appreciate that much mail from you?
- Bi-weekly.... Publishing an e-zine twice a month is just often enough to keep you fresh in your subscribers' minds but not so often that they become annoyed with you.
- Monthly... doesn't seem often enough. Your members may forget about you and where your website lives on the Internet.

8.2 Suggestion to Improve Your Membership Site

Improving and improving again your membership website is what will keep it dynamic and making a steady and reliable income. It is a law of nature (and the Internet) that everything either grows or dies. Constant improvement of your membership website will insure it grows and lives.

The content of your membership website needs to always be kept up-to-date with relevant and useful information. Keep your eyes open and all of your feelers out for information that your subscribers will find interesting and helpful. If you have always relied on only print information up to this point, try adding some audio or video. People today prefer to hear or see information rather than just to read information. Setting up audio or video feeds to your website isn't very difficult and can make a huge difference in the traffic and membership.

Each e-zine or newsletter should be filled with vital and timely information so that your subscribers eagerly await the next issue. Spend as much time and energy as you need to insure that your e-zine or newsletter isn't just deleted when it hits the in-box.

Use your auto responder to your greatest advantage. You already use it to send out emails and e-zines and newsletters. Now use it to send out vital NEWS FLASHES. Make the auto responder get the attention of your subscribers.

If you don't already have a blog, forum or message board on your membership website, then set one up as soon as possible. Members like to have input and you will benefit greatly from constructive member input. You can ask them what they would like to see on the website and then act on suggestions that are viable.

Invite a guest who is a guru in the field of your website theme to participate in an online chat discussion. Set a specific starting and stopping time and be sure to outline the discussion topics.

8.3 The Main Focus of Your Membership Site

Whatever the theme of your membership website is, it should always be your main focus. Every piece of written content, audio content or video content should be about the main theme of your membership website. Little side trips into very closely related fields is alright but even very closely related subjects should never detract from the main focus of your site.

When you chose the theme for your membership website, you chose it because it was something that you knew a lot about and/or were (and hopefully still are) passionate about.

I saw a sign in a convenience store not long ago that said something like....we strive to always be kind, considerate and helpful. However, it is hard to remember that the main objective is to drain the swamp when you are up to your ears (cleaned up) in alligators. That is true for owners of membership websites. It really is hard to stay focused on your objectives when you have so many things to distract you from doing what you need to do to keep your website focused on the main theme.

No matter how many distractions you have, you must still keep new, fresh, relevant and timely content on your website that pertains to the theme of your site.

Your e-zines and newsletters need to be filled with helpful and useful information. Be sure to continually check for new products that would be helpful to your membership. New products come out daily and you don't want to fall behind.

You need to make full use of your auto responder to keep your members informed and to keep them focused on the objective, as well.

Your blog, forum or message board topics can become unfocused and off-topic very easily. They must be monitored daily...maybe even several times each day.

8.4 Being Professional with Help Desk Systems and Forums

You need to automate everything if you want to be successful in measuring customer satisfaction. Surveying your customers is a great way of measuring customer satisfaction but if they take too much time away from other important work, it will fall by the wayside. Automate both your requests for completing the survey and your collection and reporting of the data. Some help desk management software will do this for you. If yours does not, consider customization that will enable it -- it's worth the investment.

One of the best ways to find out how effective your customers think your help desk or forum is, is to take a survey.... ask the people who actually use the help desk or forum what they think about it. Asking for suggestions to improve your help desk or forum is a good idea. There are many approaches to surveying, but some are more effective than others.

Often times membership websites will send a customer satisfaction survey of their help desk or forum to their entire list. There are several problems with this approach. First not everyone surveyed will have used your help desk's services. This will either make your percentage of responses low or add irrelevant responses to your data. Since you only request this information once in a while, you will be tempted to cram too much information into the survey. Often these surveys lack focus and do not give you a clear picture of performance.

A better approach to help desk or forum customer satisfaction measurement is case-by-case surveying. Each time a case is closed, meaning the problem was resolved and the resolution was already communicated to the requester, a short survey on the case is sent to the requester.

This is great information for continuous improvement and you can review the comments provided by your customers.

8.5 How to Manage Your Growing Members

Membership websites, while extremely diverse in the make-up of their memberships, share three common goals: attracting new members, retaining present members and successfully managing a growing membership list.

Membership websites that truly want to serve their members must constantly strive for awareness of the concerns and issues faced by membership, as well as ways for strengthening values of members and guiding members' development. But, how can that happen if management lacks understanding about what the members want?

Believe it or not, the answer is simple: ask! Find out what your members want by asking them to evaluate the website's current products and services and the manner in which the membership website provide these products and services. Survey your membership (and potential new members) regarding their opinions and attitudes.

Surveying your membership gleans all the information you need for successfully managing a growing membership website. More importantly, surveys improve member satisfaction and member profitability. Members fell like they are empowered when management listens and takes direction based on members' desires. Digging through member responses offers deep understanding of the very foundation of the membership website. This critical step in members-only website management should never be overlooked.

Some of the things that can be learned from membership surveys include:

• Demographics;
• Critical changes in members' lives;
• Members interests;
• Additional services desired;
• Newsletters and e-zines regularly read (insight for marketing to potential new members); and
• Reasons for maintaining membership.

The software you use to take surveys on your membership website should help you discover ways for retaining members, and perhaps capturing those looking at the competition, by understanding the members' needs and wants and gain critical information for directing and preparing your website for the future. The software should provide you with results that contain easy to read graphs and charts, summaries and conclusions.

CHAPTER 9:
IN CLOSING

9.1 Top Examples of Membership Sites

There are in fact only two types of membership websites. There are **free** membership sites and there are **paid** membership sites. The two types of membership sites have one thing is common. Their memberships are made up of people who share a common interest or have a common need.

Basically, a free membership website charges no membership fees. Instead the owner of the free membership website makes money by advertising and selling products and services to members while providing valuable information at no cost.

Examples of Free Membership Sites

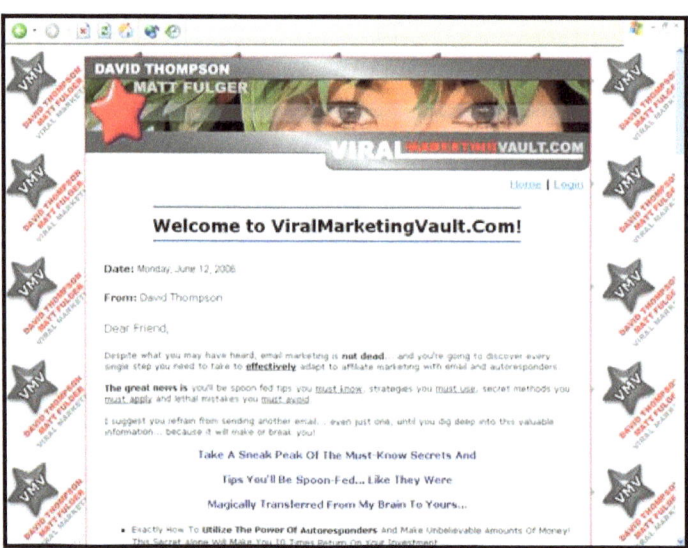

The Viral Marketing Vault: This is a free membership site, owned by David Thompson, which promises not to sell your email address and provides valuable marketing information to its members.

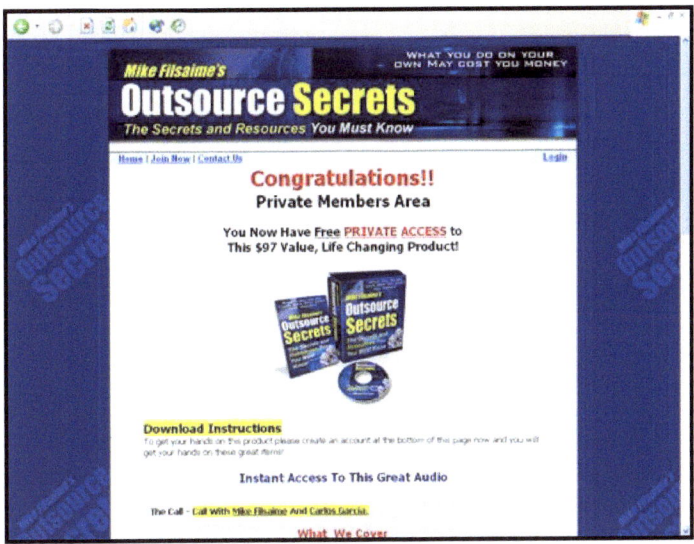

Outsource Secrets: discover the secrets of outsourcing effectively on the free membership site.

Examples of Paid Membership Sites

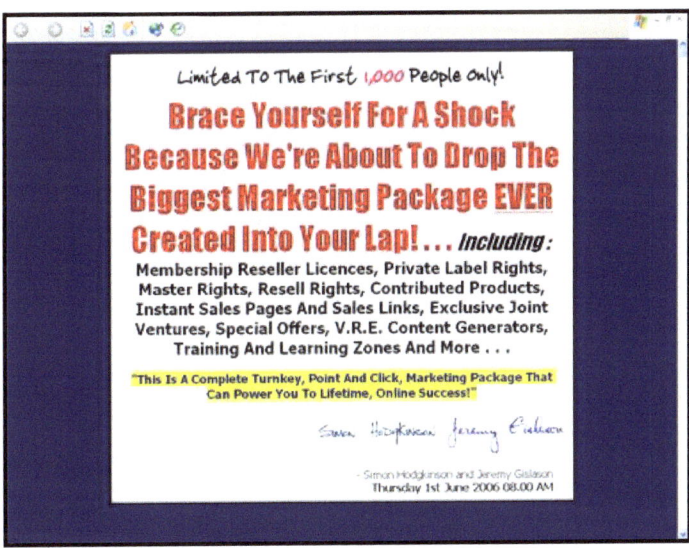

Marketing Main Event: This is by far the best example of a paid membership website dedicated to online marketing at its best and with a twist, limiting to only 1,000 memberships – tapping on exclusivity.

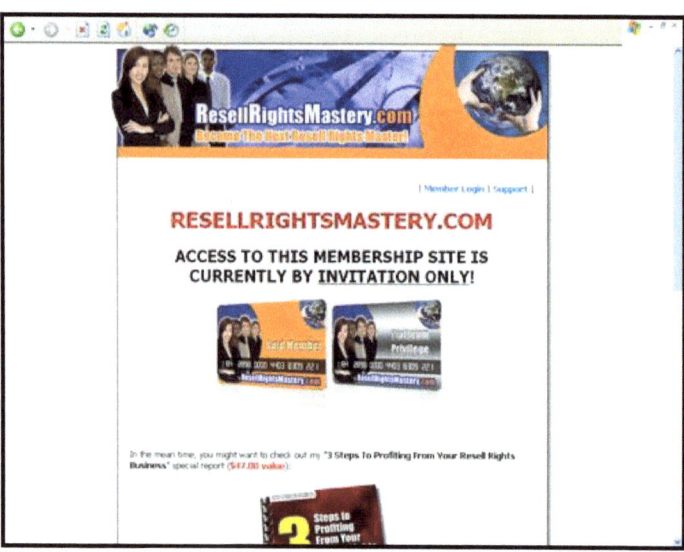

Resell Rights Mastery: This is another excellent example of a paid membership website that is marketing with a twist - the memberships are available only by invitation. This is some of the membership sites that spot more than one level (usually, 2 to 3 - sometimes 4) indicating different kind of benefits and privileges. For example: Free, Bronze, Silver, Gold, Platinum.

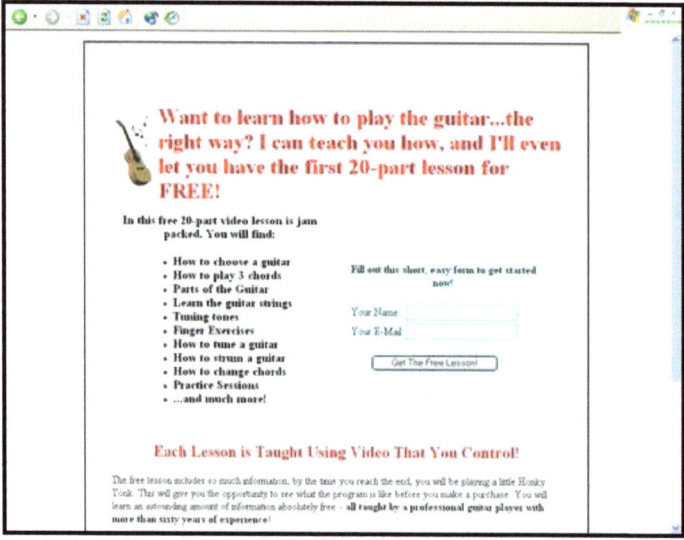

Guitar Lessons with Video: This website offers a free download that includes three open chords plus some seventh and minor chords. The full beginner course and access to a forum and blog must be bought.

9.2 Is Starting a Membership Site for You?

The Internet is the ultimate 'equal opportunity employer'. Anybody can start a membership business on the Internet. All that is needed is a subject, a website and the tools to build the site. You can start a membership website business but the question is should you?

Many people that decide to start a home based membership website business are destined to fail because their motivation and expectations are completely unrealistic. Before you attempt to start a membership website business you need to do a reality check.

First, if you really think that you can build a couple of web pages, invest little or no money, time or effort and start making an income tomorrow, you are so wrong. Building a business...any business...takes time. It also takes a monetary investment, a lot of effort and energy, and, above all else, patience, passion for the theme of the website, and a drive for success.

Almost equally important is the need to have realistic economic expectations when undertaking a home based membership website business. A home membership website internet business provides many rewards such as working in the comfort of your own home, avoiding a stressful commute, being your own boss, setting your own hours, no dress code, etc., etc., but anyone that is also expecting instant riches is sadly mistaken.

Study the opportunities of a membership website business carefully. If you have the personal traits required to succeed then select the theme that seems to fit your own particular interests or talents. What is a good choice for one person may be a very poor fit for someone else. The common thread that applies to everyone is that you must passionately believe in what you are doing and anything less than total commitment isn't enough.

9.3 Last Words and in Conclusion

The facts about starting either a free membership or paid membership website Internet business are simply that the choices must be made that are the right choices for you. Before you even consider a membership website business, ask yourself these questions:

Choice #1: Will you choose to set up a membership website business at all?

It you have the personal traits of being willing to work hard, invest your own time and money, put forth the effort, and learn from those who have gone before, then the choice is an easy 'yes' answer.

Choice #2: Will you choose to set up a free membership website or a paid membership site?

Both types will eventually bring you a good income but you must choose between them. Read and learn all you can before you make this important choice. Weigh the pros and cons of both. Do you know what kind of membership site you will choose?

Choice #3: Are you willing to invest not only your money but your time learning to use new technologies that become available?

Starting a new membership website is the beginning and not the end. Things change everyday and you must be willing to adapt to changes that will benefit your business. The only thing that will never change is that things will change. Is the answer to this question yes or no?

Choice #4: Are you good at (or willing to become good at) marketing your membership website?

Marketing is the key to success for any business and membership website businesses are not an exception to that rule. It takes some money to advertise your membership website and attract members whether it is a free or paid membership site. It also takes learning where and how to invest your marketing dollars to your best advantage. Can you answer with a firm yes?

If you answered all of the above questions with a heartfelt 'YES', then you are ready to go forward with your membership website plans.

Get started now! Make Money with Membership Sites.

Dr. Davies Mulenga

7.3 Recommended Resources

Recommended Payment Processors

<u>2CheckOut.com</u> – start accepting credit card payments from customers from several parts of the world!

<u>PayPal</u> – the most used and recognized merchant in the Internet marketplace.

Useful Website References
Traffic and Income Generating Sites:

http://www.globalonlineshop.co.uk/
http://www.getfreesoftwarefast.com
http://crowd1.com/signup/topmillionaire
http://www.webfire.com/a/?id=29029
https://www.mlmgateway.com/?refcode=82628821

https://dr-davies-school.thinkific.com/courses/
http://www.gigpanda.com
http://www.shop-for-shop.co.uk
http://www.getfreesoftwarefast.com/isf/optin.php
http://www.shop-on-shop.org/
http://www.shoppingsherlock.com/465048
http://invitation.shoppingsherlock.com/465048
http://gr8.com//pr/fE45C/d
https://udimi.com/a/ulmqo
https://amzn.to/2zWarxj
https://www.amazon.co.uk/kindle-dbs/hz/signup?tag=gloonlsho-21
https://www.amazon.com/dp/3741284165/
https://amzn.to/2rcj0CE
https://amzn.to/36HWzFU
https://dr-davies-school.thinkific.com/courses/how-to-become-an-expert-in-your-niche

7.4 Recommended Platforms to Make Money Online

Be part of the HOTTEST sector right now with Crowd1 which is exploding globally with over 1,000,000 new members in just a few short months of 2019. When you see the sector you will understand the massive affiliate income potential and why 1,000,000 is just the start. Do NOT Miss this as its hot right NOW ! http://crowd1.com/signup/topmillionaire

BEST BUSINESS GROWTH AND BUSINESS SUCCESS
Growing your Business into a Sustainable Wealth and Income Generator
https://www.bod.de/buchshop/best-business-growth-and-business-success-davies-m-mulenga-9783741284168

https://www.facebook.com/bestbusinessgrowthandbusinesssuccess/

Check out THE BEST BUSINESS GROWTH AND BUSINESS SUCCESS Growing your Business into a Sustainable Wealth and Income Generator
https://www.amazon.com/dp/3741284165/
https://amzn.to/36HWzFU
https://amzn.to/2rcj0CE

Come and join this great platform for independent business owners and network marketers. Get free leads and traffic plus massive affiliate income potential. My invitation gives you 5 free credits to begin with!
https://www.mlmgateway.com/?refcode=82628821
Visit also http://shop-on-shop.org/

Further Books from Dr. Davies Mulenga

Am frischen Wasser, Gedichte zur Erbauung der Seele
http://www.shop-on-shop.org/Tips-Advice/200/give-you-Ebook-Am-frischen-Wasser-Gedichte-zur-Erbauung-der-Seele

Zum Sulfatangriff auf Beton und Mörtel einschliesslich der Thaumasitbildung
http://shop-on-shop.org/

About the Author:

Eur Ing Dr. Davies M. Mulenga,
PhD MScEng BEng CEng MICE MVDI DBA THEOL

Formerly Structures Asset Manager on the £6,2 Billion Pounds Motorway Project in London UK, Dr Davies Mulenga is Managing Director in Germany, a chartered Civil Structural Engineer, Pastor and bestseller co-author. Also, Principal Structures Consultant Dr Mulenga has worked as expert advisor on several high profile multi-million Pound projects in Europe and overseas. A game changer with over 25 years of remarkable experience in Engineering including Business and Asset Management.

He has also taught in Universities and stands as one of the most successful business and engineering talents of all time. Website: http://www.getfreesoftwarefast.com

Thank You for Reading!